The Road Back

Endangered Species Recovery

Success with Partners

Dedication

Mollie H. Beattie
Volunteer Inc

"Our fate and that of our economy
are linked to natural systems. We
cannot eliminate species and expect
our own
to survive."

Mollie H. Beattie
Director, U.S. Fish and
Wildlife Service
1993-1996

Front Cover:
Peregrine Falcon
P. Hollis/USFWS

This report is dedicated to Mollie Beattie, the former Director of the Fish and Wildlife Service, who lost her personal struggle with brain cancer on June 27, 1996. During her three-year tenure as Director, Mollie challenged the Service to adopt an ecosystem approach to fulfill its conservation mission. She believed that this approach, supported by the development of new partnerships and the strengthening of old ones, would assure success. Mollie dedicated her life to conserving wildlife and the ecosystems that support them. She worked tirelessly to make the Endangered Species Act work better, because she believed that Aldo Leopold was correct: 'The first rule of intelligent tinkering is to save all the parts.'

Restoring a threatened or endangered species to a secure status is seldom an easy process. It requires the cooperation and involvement of a wide array of interests, including Federal, State, and local agencies; Tribal governments; scientists from a variety of disciplines; conservation organizations; the business community; landowners, and other concerned individuals. Without their help, the successes described in this report could not have been achieved. This report was made possible by the many people who shared their ideas, species accounts, and beautiful photographs, and by Mollie Beattie.

The Road Back

These Peregrine falcon chicks, shown nesting in the wild, are examples of successful recovery efforts.
Karen Bollinger/USFWS

Endangered Species Recovery

Success with Partners

Recovery of the Shasta crayfish depends on healthy river habitats.
US FWS

Aquatic ecosystems are home to approximately 40 percent of listed species, highlighting the need for clean water.

Contents

Introduction

America's landscape has undergone dramatic changes over the past 300 years. The towering forests and vast prairies that once characterized the landscape now are crisscrossed by highways and fragmented by cities and towns. The environment has changed rapidly because of the increasing demands of the growing human population for water, land, and energy to support agriculture, industry, transportation, and other interests. These changes are stressing many of our natural communities and the native plant and animal species they sustain. As a result, many species have gone extinct, while others are threatened with a similar fate.

Recognizing these alarming trends, Congress took action in 1973, by passing the Endangered Species Act (Act). This significant legislation reflects the deep respect and appreciation that Americans have for our natural resources, as well as an understanding that all life is linked to a healthy environment. The Act has been credited with saving hundreds of species from extinction, including the California condor and the black-footed ferret, and for improving the quality of habitat for many more common species.

Our national symbol, the bald eagle, is a good example of the progress achieved under the Act. This magnificent bird once nested throughout the United States. By 1967, however, the species was eliminated from much of its range, and the number of bald eagles in the lower 48 States had dropped to only 417 nesting pairs. Declines in the population were attributed to habitat loss, illegal shooting, and the effects of DDT (a widely-used pesticide) on its reproduction. Efforts that have led to the species' successful recovery include protecting nesting sites, reestablishing young eagles into former habitat, rehabilitating injured eagles, banning DDT, and other actions involving the public and private sectors. These recovery efforts helped to boost the current eagle population in the lower 48 States to more than 4,000 nesting pairs. The success of these efforts allowed the Service to upgrade the status of the eagle from endangered to threatened in 1995.

Facing Page: Much of the California gnatcatcher's habitat has been changed through economic development near cities.
Claire Dobert/USFWS

Right: Bald eagles can now be seen throughout much of their former range because of collaborative recovery efforts.
Jeff Foott/USFWS

Large areas of desert tortoise habitat have been protected through cooperative efforts.
Jim Fisher/USFWS

Desert Tortoise

The Service is cooperating with the Bureau of Land Management to conduct numerous recovery actions for the desert tortoise. These include monitoring permanent study plots to learn about long-term population trends of the tortoise and sponsoring conferences to develop desert management practices. In addition, the Bureau of Land Management is managing its desert tortoise habitat to ensure the species' long-term protection. Research on nutrition and foraging ecology, being conducted by the Bureau of Land Management, has already been used by the Service to develop the Desert Tortoise Recovery Plan.

Desert tortoise
Luke or Golden ????/USFWS

What is the Endangered Species Act?

The Act, regarded as one of the world's most important wildlife conservation laws, calls for conserving threatened and endangered plants and animals and the ecosystems (or habitats) on which they depend. The Act defines "conserve" as restoring species to a point where their populations are stable and no longer in need of special protection. Congress envisioned a network of international, national, State and local governments, as well as industry, conservation groups, and private individuals, working together toward the common goal of conserving and recovering species. The Act establishes a leadership role for the Federal Government in conserving and recovering species at risk. The U.S. Fish and Wildlife Service and the National Marine Fisheries Service (NMFS) are responsible for the administration of the Act and for the coordination of recovery efforts for species. The Service is responsible for terrestrial and most freshwater species, while NMFS is responsible for marine species and anadromous fish, such as salmon and the Hawaiian monk seal.

The Service, through its recovery program and with cooperators, works to stabilize, conserve, and recover listed species by securing their populations, reversing declining numbers, and stabilizing species so that they are no longer in danger of extinction. The participation of Federal, State, and local agencies, Tribal governments, conservation organizations, the business community, landowners, and other concerned citizens has been critical to the stabilization and recovery of these plants and animals.

Red cockaded woodpecker poises at the entrance to one of the nest cavities developed as part of a recovery effort.
USFWS

Red-Cockaded Woodpecker

The focus of conserving red-cockaded woodpeckers on non-federal lands is to build incentives for conservation by providing a simple mechanism for small woodlot owners to effectively work with small groups of birds. The Service must demonstrate to private landowners the importance of their role in recovery, which is to help increase the population on unoccupied habitat on federal lands in areas where there are designated recovery populations.

Sixty seven percent of the freshwater mussels are rare or imperiled, and one out of every 10 mussel species may have become extinct during this century alone.

Ozark Cavefish

Partnership efforts between government agencies and private organizations have protected several populations of Ozark cavefish in Benton County, Arkansas, since this species was listed as threatened in 1984. This blind, translucent fish is found in caves within the central portions of the Ozark Highlands in Arkansas, Missouri, and Oklahoma. Several private landowners, working with this alliance of agencies, have agreed voluntarily to protect caves and to help improve the groundwater on their land to assist the species. Through these efforts, several populations of Ozark cavefish have been protected in Benton County, Arkansas.

Ozark cavefish habitat has been protected through voluntary agreements with landowners.
USFWS

What Types of Activities Threaten Listed Species?

Although people have been altering the natural environment for thousands of years, technological advances and accelerated development of the past few centuries have drastically changed many natural habitats. Many human activities have had serious detrimental effects on species, including:

+ land-clearing activities for agricultural production, homes, shopping malls, and reservoirs;

+ the pollution of our air, water, and land;

+ collection of species for commercial, recreational, or educational purposes; and

+ introduction of nonnative species and diseases into our environment.

In almost every case, these human activities were not meant to harm wildlife and plants, but nonetheless, the resulting effects have pushed some species to the brink of extinction.

Knowlton Cactus

A second reintroduced population of the Knowlton cactus is being established, and there currently are 69 seedlings produced from seeds from the first site. The Service, State of New Mexico, and Bureau of Land Management all have participated in this project.

A new Knowlton cactus seedling now can be seen because of the recovery efforts that involved the Service, the State of New Mexico, and the Bureau of Land Management.
USFWS

Coastal marsh restoration is just one type of recovery activity implemented to restore habitat to benefit a variety of species, like the Yuma clapper rail.
USFWS

One of the Service's Partners for Wildlife projects, shown in the two photos taken one year apart, has been completed along the Clinch River in southwestern Virginia. Under a voluntary agreement, private land adjacent to the river was fenced to protect the riparian zone from livestock grazing, which subsequently reduced the amount of runoff from surrounding agricultural uses. Protection of this habitat benefited several species of endangered freshwater mussels and fish species at risk.

The successes of these cooperative recovery efforts are demonstrated by the fact that approximately 60 percent of the species listed between 1968 and 1973 are known currently to be stable or improving in status.

Partners from around the world participate in green sea turtle recovery efforts.
Gary Stormo/USFWS

Why Save Threatened and Endangered Species?

Economics: Economic benefits provided by a plant or animal species are lost if the species becomes extinct. For example, the chinook salmon population in the Pacific Northwest has supported valuable commercial and recreational fisheries, providing food and generating jobs and income for many people. Any decline in the salmon populations means a decline in the number of fish that can be harvested, resulting in an economic loss.

Medicine: Nature is a storehouse of potential medicines that can be used to treat a wide variety of diseases. Approximately 50 percent of prescribed medicines are derived from substances found in plants and animals. The Pacific yew tree, for example, provides an anti-cancer substance, the rosy periwinkle yields drugs to treat childhood leukemia, and the foxglove plant provides digitalis, an important heart medicine. Recently, a new cancer medication was developed from a compound isolated from the Asian mayapple, which is found only in India and Pakistan and is imperiled. If species become extinct before they are studied, their chemical secrets will disappear with them.

Agriculture: Thomas Jefferson wrote that "the greatest service which can be rendered any country is to add a useful plant to its culture, especially a grain." Botanists estimate that, of the more than 30,000 species of edible plants, less than 20 produce 90 percent of the world's food. Plant collectors currently are seeking out remaining wild strains of crops, such as wheat and corn that can be used to develop hybrid species that are more resistant to crop diseases, pests, and marginal climatic conditions. Also, chemists recently found a compound derived from the endangered Archbold mint that is highly repellant to insects.

Aesthetic/Spiritual: Species and their ecosystems provide essential aesthetic, spiritual, and quality-of-life values to the citizens of our country and its visitors. Many religions teach stewardship of the Earth and respect for nature as God's creation.

Recreational: "Eco-tourism," a new industry developing throughout the world, is based on the fact that many people are willing to pay for the chance to experience nature, including native plants and animals. An increasing number of people are planning their vacations around the enjoyment of wildlife or wildlife activities, such as whale watching. In 1991, an estimated 76 million people in the United States participated in bird-related recreation.

Species of plants and animals are sometimes compared to books in a library. Conservation ensures that the libraries we leave our children will not be empty, but instead will be full of secrets that can be unlocked, discovered, and enjoyed for years to come. Nobody knows which species may be essential in the future or what is lost when a species goes extinct. But one thing is certain: Extinction is Forever. Why should we save endangered and threatened plants and animals? **BECAUSE WE CAN.**

Tan Riffleshell

A coordinated recovery effort among the Service, other Federal, State, and local agencies, conservation organizations, and individual citizens has set the stage for implementing recovery activities for the tan riffleshell mussel. A recent mollusk survey discovered two populations of this endangered mussel. The populations were healthy and rebounding and were found to be reproducing. Additional research efforts on the species' life history is essential to its recovery. The Service is reaching out to other partners, especially local agencies, individuals, and organizations to enlist their support in protecting this species by restoring the stream habitat and water quality that it requires.

Florida Scrub Jay

Habitat protection through land acquisition has made a major contribution to the recovery of the threatened Florida scrub jay. A cooperative effort among the Service, National Aeronautics and Space Administration, National Park Service, and the State of Florida in conducting habitat surveys and managing habitats for scrub jays on public lands is helping to conserve the species. The National Aeronautics and Space Administration has banded nearly all scrub jays on Kennedy Space Center property, and research is being conducted on the biology of the species to help ensure its long-term survival. Private landowners, through the habitat conservation planning process, are critical partners in the conservation of this Florida species.

Florida scrub jay populations are being protected through the habitat conservation planning process currently being implemented in the Southeast.
USFWS

Seventy two percent of the species listed as of September 30, 1996, have final recovery plans; an additional 12 percent have draft plans that outline recovery strategies.

The Service, along with numerous cooperators is developing a Multi Species Recovery Plan to address the recovery of all federally listed species in the South Florida Ecosystem.
Richard Frear/National Park Service

Recovery: What Does it Mean?

Recovery is the process by which the decline of an endangered or threatened species is reversed, the threats to its survival are overcome, and the species is restored to a point that its population in the wild is healthy and secure. The goal of recovery is to restore the species so that extinction is no longer a threat. Typically, recovering a species is a gradual process that may take years.

Recovery plans, which are documents that summarize threats, and identify a series of actions to conserve or recover the species, begin the recovery process. Recovery plans serve as blueprints for private, Federal and State cooperation in the conservation of species and the ecosystems on which they depend. Teams that draft recovery plans include biologists familiar with the species. In addition, teams often feature representatives of affected communities and industries, major landowners, and other people with expertise and an interest in the species. Coordination among Federal, State, and local agencies, conservation organizations, species experts, and affected private individuals is a key ingredient for effective recovery plan development and implementation. The recovery planning process is designed to allow potentially affected segments of the public to participate in decision making and allows the special local knowledge of affected communities to be fully considered. Draft plans then are made available for public review and comment, and all affected or interested individuals and groups are encouraged to participate. Federal, State, and private agencies and organizations may be identified in recovery plans as having opportunities to undertake various recovery tasks. While the plans do not require that these actions be taken, they do lay out a coordinated strategy for reaching recovery goals. Strategies outlined in recovery plans may be modified when needed to incorporate new information and ensure that species remain on the most effective path to recovery.

Recognizing that listed species may share similar habitats and face similar threats, the Service is developing recovery plans that combine recovery activities for several listed and sensitive species whenever possible. This "multispecies" or "ecosystem" approach is often more efficient, thus decreasing the recovery costs and increasing the effectiveness of the recovery actions. The Service, in cooperation with NMFS, the Florida Game and Fresh Water Fish Commission, State agencies, local governments, the academic community, conservation organizations, and private entities, is preparing a Multi-Species Recovery Strategy to address the recovery needs of all federally-listed threatened and endangered species in the South Florida Ecosystem. This recovery strategy will be one of the first recovery plans that is specifically designed to meet the needs of multiple species that do not occupy similar habitats. It also will be one of the first recovery plans that is designed to approach recovery by addressing the needs of an entire watershed, in this case, the critical Kissimmee-Okeechobee-Everglades Watershed. In addition to the 68 federally listed species, the Multi-Species Recovery Strategy will address the recovery needs of the two candidates for federal listing, species listed by the State of Florida, and other sensitive species, such as the over 400 species of migratory birds, that depend on the South Florida ecosystem.

A conservation agreement between land managers in Utah for protection of the endangered Virgin River chub and woundfin also protects habitat for the Virgin River spinedace and many other species. The conservation agreement resulted in the Service being able to withdraw the proposal to list the Virgin River spinedace.
USFWS

What Kind of Recovery Activities Can Help a Listed Species?

The specific actions needed to restore a plant or animal to a secure status vary from species to species. Some may be as simple as gating the entrance to a cave to protect specific habitat for an endangered bat or cave fish. Other activities may be more complex and lengthy, requiring extensive cooperation among State and Federal agencies, Tribal governments, independent groups, and individuals to ensure their successful completion.

Examples of recovery activities include:

+ Plant propagation efforts for 10 critically endangered plants from Kauai, Hawaii, have greatly enhanced their chances for recovery thanks to a National Tropical Botanical Garden project funded by the Service;

+ Captive breeding has produced California condors, whooping cranes, red wolves, and black-footed ferrets for release back into their historic range;

+ Record numbers of Puerto Rican parrot chicks have been produced during the last three breeding seasons through implementation of nest enhancement procedures.

Indiana Bat

The Service coordinated the construction of a bat conservation gate to protect a New Jersey cave that is an important bat wintering site. This gate protects the vulnerable cave from intruders, while still allowing the bats to come and go as needed. This project was a partnership effort between the Service, the New Jersey Department of Environmental Protection, Bat Conservation International, and the American Cave Conservation Association. In addition, two new populations of bats were discovered because of an intensive survey at military installations and two large tracts of forest. A summer roosting area and a nursery habitat have also been preserved.

Nobody knows which
species may be
essential in the future
or what is lost when a
species goes extinct,
but one thing is
certain: Extinction
is Forever.

Why is Recovery a Complex and Challenging Endeavor?

Many of the reasons for a species' decline are the result of as much as 300 years of habitat destruction and degradation. Just as threats accumulate through time, reversing them also requires time. Options for restoring habitat that a species depends on may be limited because of competing needs and uses.

One way to think about recovery is to view it as a puzzle with pieces that need to be placed skillfully together to ensure the species is secure and will continue to survive in years to come. Because of the unique biological requirements and the many threats to the species, the road to recovery for each species is different. Federal agency coordination, public participation, grants to the States, recovery tasks implementation, and recovery or species agreements are some of the pieces that make recovery a reality.

Scientists estimate that more than 500 species in the United States slipped into extinction during the 300 years before the Act was passed.

The Tooth Cave spider is part of a unique cave ecosystem that is being preserved in the Texas hill country.
Marcos Huerta/USFWS

How do Cooperative Partnerships Assist with Recovery?

Recovery of threatened and endangered species depends on a network of Federal, State and private organizations, and individuals working in partnership with the Service. A 1993 study by the Association for Biodiversity Information and The Nature Conservancy revealed interesting statistics about listed species populations. Only twenty-five percent of all listed species occur primarily on Federal lands. In addition, more than half of the listed species have at least 80% of their habitat on private lands. Therefore, recovering endangered species requires partnerships with people who manage the non-federal lands. Many partnerships already have been developed to help coordinate recovery efforts for listed species, but there is still more work to be done. There are numerous examples that illustrate how these partnerships have helped to conserve or recover species and their habitats, including:

California least tern: Threats such as habitat disturbance had reduced the California least tern to a low of 625 pairs in 1973. Recovery efforts, including habitat protection and management, have since led to an increase in the population to at least 2,400 pairs. Partners essential to this successful recovery program include the California Department of Parks and Recreation, the Department of the Navy, and the University of California.

Small-whorled pogonia: Residential and commercial development have been the primary threats to the small whorled pogonia. However, since the plant's listing, State and municipal conservation efforts and private landowner contributions have afforded permanent protection for the largest-known population of this plant, allowing it to be reclassified as threatened.

Partners in Flight Program: Initiated by the Service, this program focuses on conserving imperiled birds and restoring their habitat and includes about 90 cooperators in three countries from Federal and State agencies, non-governmental organizations, and industry. The program not only helps imperiled birds, but benefits other species that depend on the same habitat. Habitat conservation alliances like these can decrease the need to list species, because their efforts focus on conserving species and their habitat before they are listed. Many recovery activities that aid in conserving and recovering species can be implemented through these cooperative ventures or alliances.

Populations of the prairie fringed orchid have been stabilized, in part because of recovery efforts such as this research project.
USFWS

How Can Landowners Become Involved?

Cooperative partnerships aren't just for government agencies and other large groups. Private landowners are essential to the conservation and recovery of many listed plants and animals, especially when you consider that more than 700 species are known to occur on private or non-Federal lands. A simple action, such as placing a fence next to a stream to eliminate grazing along the banks, thus reducing erosion, could require little time or money, but may be critical to the survival of a listed plant, fish, or mussel. For example, the Minnesota Department of Agriculture works with hundreds of private landowners who are willing to adopt land-use practices to benefit rare species, such as changing the use of pesticides on their lands. Some private individuals act as voluntary caretakers of the Minnesota dwarf trout lily after the species was discovered on their land. Other landowners are protecting habitat for the threatened Western prairie fringed orchid through voluntary landowner agreements and efforts by the State. The land where this species is found has been protected, and populations have been stabilized.

All 50 States, as well as U.S. territories and commonwealths, have entered into cooperative agreements with the Service to conserve threatened and endangered species.

Wyoming Toad

The Wyoming toad is benefiting greatly from restrictions on pesticide use within its native habitat. In addition, an intensive survey program is being conducted to try to find additional populations and habitat. These recovery activities are the result of a cooperative effort among concerned organizations.

Loggerhead Sea Turtle

Recovery efforts are helping protect sea turtles by monitoring nest sites, limiting structures that hinder sea turtle nesting, and reducing artificial lighting used near beaches at night. (Lights cause both adult and newly hatched sea turtles to become disoriented.) The Florida Department of Natural Resources has conducted workshops for private, State, and Federal personnel to teach them how to assess sea turtle nesting success.

The Florida Department of Natural Resources also implements regulations designed to protect sea turtles on the beach and in the water, conducts research on sea turtle ecology, and oversees research conducted by other agencies or individuals. The Center for Marine Conservation and the Caribbean Conservation Corporation assist in funding the Archie Carr National Wildlife Refuge (one of the areas preserved for the turtles) reviewing measures proposed to protect sea turtles, and seeking public support for such measures.

What Successes have been Achieved?

Recovery of threatened and endangered species is a tremendous challenge, but it is doable, and the successes are much celebrated by the American public. Of all the species listed between 1968 and 1993, only seven, or less than one percent, have been officially recognized as extinct. Preventing the extinction of the remaining 99 percent is perhaps the biggest success story of the Act. This success is attributed to the efforts of other Federal agencies, States, Tribal governments, private organizations, and individuals working with the Service towards a common goal. The Service and its partners in recovery are collecting biological information, developing recovery strategies, and implementing management activities that will stabilize, halt, or reverse the trends towards extinction. There are numerous successes in these efforts. A few follow.

American Peregrine Falcon

Nesting precariously on high cliff faces and diving at speeds in excess of 200 mph to capture prey, this magnificent American bird is an indicator of the overall health of its environment. However, it all-but-succumbed to pesticide contamination (which caused thinning of eggshells and adult mortality) in the early 1970's. Declines in this species' population were also attributed to habitat loss and illegal shooting. The falcon has benefited greatly from cooperative recovery efforts, such as the ban on the pesticide DDT and broad-based public involvement. More than 3,400 young

falcons were released into the wild through nationwide recovery efforts. The release of these falcons and other recovery activities have helped to stabilize the falcon's population to the point where it no longer may need protection of the Act.

Widespread public involvement has helped lead to dramatic increases in American peregrine falcon populations.
Skip Ambrose/USFWS

Recovery efforts have increased black-footed ferret numbers from 18 to more than 400.
Rich Reagan/USFWS

Greenback cutthroat trout recovery efforts have restored this species to more than 40 lakes and streams.
Erwin Boeker/USFWS

Black-footed Ferret

The black-footed ferret formerly lived throughout the Great Plains from Alberta, Canada, south to northern Texas and eastern Arizona, and with its primary prey, the prairie dog, was an important species in this ecosystem. Prairie dog control programs, which reduced the ferret's food source, greatly impacted the populations of the black-footed ferret. Once thought to be extinct, black-footed ferrets were rediscovered in 1981 near Meeteetse, Wyoming. A captive breeding program, founded by the 18 survivors of this population, has been extremely successful, resulting in a population of more than 400 by mid-1992. In the fall of 1991, 49 juvenile ferrets were released in the Shirley Basin area of southeast Wyoming. The release was the result of considerable landowner cooperation, because about 55 percent of the management area where the ferrets were released is in private ownership. Similar releases were conducted in north-central Montana and the Conata Basin/ Badlands area of South Dakota in 1994. In the fall of 1996, family groups of ferrets (including pups whelped that summer) were released into the Aubrey Valley in northern Arizona. Releases continue at all sites. Now, there are young born in the wild, too!

Greenback Cutthroat Trout

Over millions of years, a diversity of trout species evolved across the West, each adapted to the unique characteristics of the streams and lakes that they inhabited. One of these, the greenback cutthroat trout, is a species that is both extremely beautiful and a challenging sport fish. This native cutthroat trout declined, because of overharvest, widespread destruction of habitat, and the introduction of nonnative trout into its native streams. At the time of its listing, only two small populations were known to exist. Efforts to conserve those populations and recover the species started in 1959 through a cooperative effort by the Bureau of Land Management, Colorado State University, the Service, Forest Service, National Park Service, and the Colorado Division of Endangered Species. Establishing new populations of the greenback cutthroat involved removing nonnative fish, restoring habitat, and regulating fishing. Since it was listed in 1967, the species has been restored in more than 40 lakes and streams in Colorado, and there is catch and release fishing for the species in 15 lakes. The species is nearing its recovery goals, and with continued reintroduction into its native streams and control of nonnative trout, the species may soon be delisted.

Louisiana Black Bear

The Louisiana black bear once roamed throughout the towering bottomland forests and wetlands of the Mississippi River Delta. By 1980, more than 80 percent of the historical habitat of the Louisiana black bear was gone, and breeding populations existed only in the Tensas and Atchafalaya river basins. Today, it is threatened because of habitat loss due to the conversion of bottomland hardwoods into open agriculture lands. Recovery efforts have been initiated by the Black Bear Conservation Committee (BBCC), a broad coalition of about 50 State and Federal agencies, forest and agricultural companies, various special interest organizations, and universities. Since its formation, the BBCC has published both the Black Bear Management Handbook and a comprehensive Black Bear Restoration Plan. A full-time coordinator has been hired to focus on public education and outreach. The BBCC has been instrumental in promoting support for black bear restoration and recovery. The BBCC also ensures that forest management activities include those that support a sustained yield of timber products and wildlife habitats, thereby maintaining forest land conditions necessary for bear recovery. This alliance is a major key to continued successful recovery efforts for the Louisiana black bear and its habitat.

The Louisiana black bear benefits from forest management practices that also support timber product harvest.
Theresa Rabot/USFWS

Aleutian Canada Goose

Smaller than most of its relatives, the Aleutian Canada goose nests primarily in meadows and marshes on the Aleutian and Kuril Islands off the coast of Alaska and winter along the Pacific Coast of the Lower United States. It is a symbol of the fragile Arctic ecosystem. In the late 1700's, fur farmers began to introduce Arctic foxes on various islands. The Aleutian Canada goose populations began to decline because the introduced foxes killed the geese. Buldir Island was the only place not invaded by foxes, allowing its geese to survive. When the Act was passed in 1973, the States of Alaska, California, and Oregon, along with the private sector and the Federal government, began recovery efforts for the species. The three main parts of the recovery strategy include: removing foxes and restoring geese to the islands, protecting geese from hunting pressures, and securing the winter habitat of the geese. Implementation of these strategies have caused an increase in the populations to approximately 7,900 birds.

Aleutian Canada geese have responded so well to recovery activities that the species' status was reclassified in 1990 from endangered to the less critical category of threatened.

Cheat Mountain Salamander

The rich hardwood forest is a delicate ecosystem in the West Virginia mountains, and contain many of nature's treasures among the tall poplar, oak, and maple trees. A lot of people would not see a salamander as a treasure. The Cheat Mountain salamander, is part of the delicate ecosystem that is threatened by human disturbance. The prospects for this species look relatively bright despite drastic historical

Thanks to successful recovery efforts, the Aleutian Canada goose is no longer endangered.
USFWS

Cooperative management protects 95 percent of known Cheat Mountain salamander populations.
Craig Stihler/WV Department of Natural Resources

decreases in the range of the Cheat Mountain salamander. Sixty-three known populations of this amphibian exist today, and approximately 95 percent of these known populations are on protected lands, primarily National Forests. The populations are not quite stable and appear to be susceptible to drought, reduction of forest canopy by storms, competition with other salamanders, and pollution, such as acid rain and snow. Protection has been provided to the salamanders through the movement or modification of proposed roads, trails, and timber harvests throughout its native habitat. As part of the recovery effort, numerous areas of the Monongahela National Forest are being surveyed for salamanders. Three quarters of the populations identified as necessary for recovery of the Cheat Mountain salamander are being protected and managed through the cooperative efforts of the State of West Virginia, the Service, and the Forest Service. Additional habitat of the Cheat Mountain salamander also was protected in 1994 as a result of the establishment of the Canaan Valley National Wildlife Refuge.

The Florida manatee is being protected through multi agency habitat protection and law enforcement efforts.
USFWS

Northeastern Beach Tiger Beetle

An entire ecosystem of specialized plants and animals evolved along the sandy beaches and dunes of our eastern seaboard. Today, the northeastern beach tiger beetle and several other species are threatened because so little undeveloped beach remains. A project to develop and field test a translocation technique using larvae of the northeastern beach tiger beetle was undertaken at the Gateway National Recreation Area, Sandy Hook Unit. The effort, conducted by the Service in cooperation with Randolph-Macon College, National Park Service, and the New Jersey Department of Environmental Protection, was the first step in determining a successful technique to be used for future reintroductions of the beetle.

During a 1995 survey of the reintroduction sites, 55 adult northeastern beach tiger beetles were found, confirming that reintroduced larvae were able to overwinter successfully and emerge as adults. Adult beetles displayed normal behavior; both feeding and mating were observed. In mid-September, 21 larvae were discovered at Sandy Hook near the area where the adult beetles had been abundant during the summer survey. This discovery indicated that the emerged adults had mated successfully and laid eggs, and that the larval young had survived. Future reintroductions using this successful technique will help recover the species.

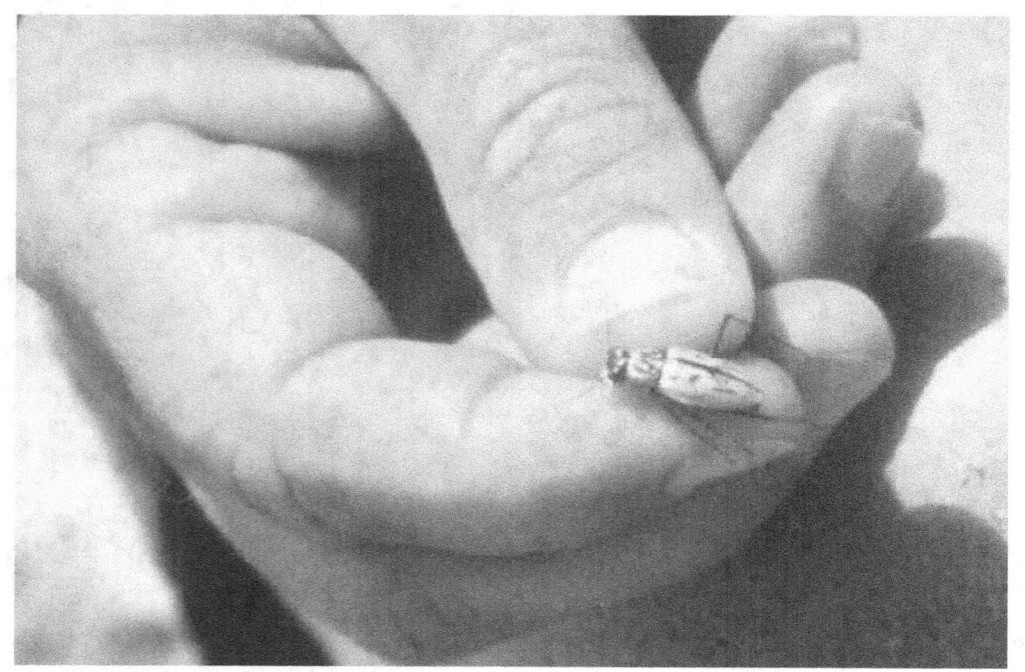

Northeastern beach tiger beetle is reintroduced into its native habitat at Sandy Hook, NJ.
Annette H. Scherer/USFWS

The northeastern beach tiger beetle are mating successfully after reintroduction.
Annette H. Scherer/USFWS

Haleakala Silversword

Island ecosystems provide unique opportunities to study the evolution of species. Hawaii is a natural laboratory with many species, such as the beautiful Haleakala silversword, that are found no where else in the world. This species of silversword is found only in a 250-acre area in the crater and on the outer slopes of Haleakala, a dormant volcano on the island of Maui, Hawaii. Population declines were attributed to habitat disturbances, detrimental effects from introduced species, and vandalism. The Haleakala National Park was established to aid in the conservation of the species. Although this eliminated some of the threats, others continued, and the silversword was listed in 1991. Now, the most dangerous threat is the loss of the plant's native pollinators, which are being threatened by the Argentine ant, an introduced species that preys on native insects. Biologists are working to find an effective control for the ants. A collaborative effort with the Park Service has saved the species from extinction, but challenges remain.

Ongoing Haleakala silversword research is addressing the remaining threats to this species.
M. Shaffer/USFWS

At this time, fewer
than 1 percent of the
world's 250,000
flowering plants
have been analyzed
to determine whether
they
hold the key to a
new medicine or cure
for human diseases.

Peter's Mountain Mallow

Peter's Mountain mallow now is restricted to a single site in the wild, a mountainous tract of land in southwestern Virginia owned by The Nature Conservancy. The species declined drastically over the past two decades, and by 1991, only three adult plants remained in the wild. The decline of Peter's Mountain mallow has been attributed to many factors, including overgrazing by large mammals, such as deer and feral goats, excessive plant collection by wildflower enthusiasts, and lack of fire. The heat of fire breaks dormancy in Peter's Mountain mallow seeds by rupturing the hard seed coat and making seeds permeable to water. Fire also eliminates competing vegetation and increases light and nutrients for the plants, thereby enhancing seedling survival and contributing to flower and fruit production.

The U.S. Forest Service and Virginia Department of Forestry provided the technical assistance necessary to conduct controlled burns in the springs of 1992-1994 at the Nature Conservancy Preserve. Seeds germinated and grew after each of these prescribed burns. In the autumn of 1995, 49 Peter's Mountain mallow plants were found in the wild because of fire management and restoration efforts.

Another recovery effort includes the work done by botanists from Virginia Polytechnic Institute and State University, who were able to find viable seeds in the leaf litter on Peter's Mountain and germinate them by using fire. These seedlings then were used to establish a garden population that produced many more seeds, allowing study of the germination and seed set problems occurring in the natural population. The Virginia Department of Conservation and Recreation's Division of Natural Heritage also designed and implemented prescribed fire research and seedling establishment at the natural population site and in experimental gardens.

Gray Wolf

Gray wolves were once common throughout most of North America. But by 1930, they had been all but wiped out in the United States outside of Alaska due to predator-control efforts. In 1967, the Gray wolf was listed as endangered in the 48 contiguous states, except for Minnesota, because of the very low numbers and threats from continued hunting and habitat loss. In 1990, a committee was established by Congress to address reintroduction of wolves into Yellowstone and central Idaho, where the largest blocks of wolf habitat remained. The reintroduction effort required the cooperation of many groups, including the Service, the U.S. Park Service, the U.S. Forest Service, the States of Montana, Wyoming and Idaho, environmental interests, timber, mining and grazing organizations, and local communities. Their efforts culminated in 1995 in the first releases of wolves into Yellowstone National Park and Idaho wilderness areas.

In 1995 and 1996, 31 Canadian wolves were released into Yellowstone National Park, and 35 were released into central Idaho. Although a few of these wolves were lost to accidents and interactions with humans, most immediately adapted to their new homes. They are doing so well that the Service recently announced that no further introductions should be necessary. In 1996, five Yellowstone packs are known to have denned, with at least 22 pups produced. And in 1997, 10 pairs are maintaining dens. The central Idaho wolves also have had great breeding success, with at least seven litters in 1996 and nine or more dens expected in 1997.

Service Director Mollie Beattie and Interior Secretary Bruce Babbitt participate in a wolf release.
USFWS

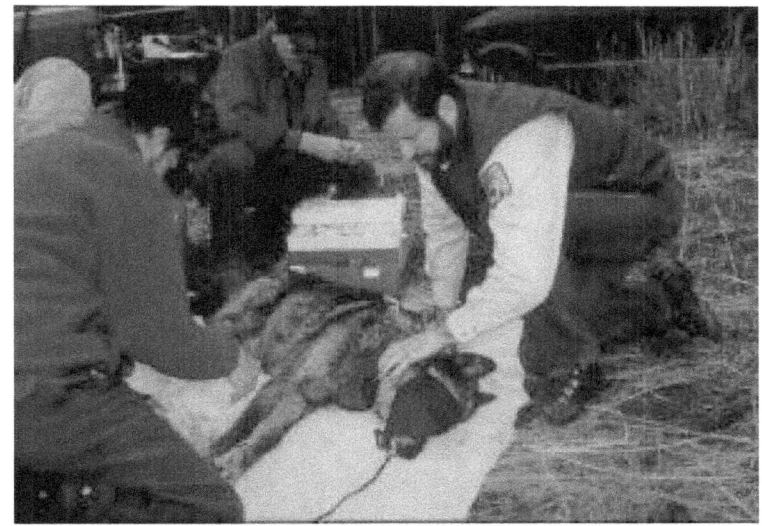

A wolf gets a radio collar and health check before being released.
USFWS

Facing Page:
The gray wolf once again roams free in Yellowstone National Park after a 50 year absence.
Tracy Brooks/Mission Wolf

Thirty seven percent
of the freshwater
fish species are at
risk of extinction,
and 35 percent of
amphibians that
depend on aquatic or
wetland habitats are
rare or imperiled.

Abrams Creek Threatened and Endangered Fish

A major recovery effort is underway in Abrams Creek, Tennessee, for the endangered smoky madtom and duskytail darter and the threatened yellowfin madtom and the spotfin chub. An alliance of numerous agencies and the private sector is coordinating recovery activities in this creek. This alliance includes the Service, Trout Unlimited, National Park Service, U.S. Forest Service, Tennessee Valley Authority, North Carolina Wildlife Resource Agency, Tennessee Wildlife Resource Agency, Conservation Fisheries Inc., University of Tennessee, and private citizens. One of the recovery activities began in 1986 as a project to restore native fish to Abrams Creek. The project is being funded by grants from the government, in-kind services, and private donations. For the first two years, the recovery activities were directed at collecting individuals from three of the four fish species in their natural habitats for use in captive breeding. Collection of the duskytail darter started in 1992. The captive breeding programs continue to produce individuals that can be stocked into their native habitats. These reintroduced fish then are monitored within the streams by biologists using snorkels.

In 1993, the National Park Service initiated another cooperative effort with the help of numerous other agencies to improve water quality in Abrams Creek and promote species recovery. Riparian vegetation has been planted, cattle have been fenced from streams, and water quality has been improved and now is monitored regularly along with the aquatic community.

After all of these efforts, the fish are showing signs of recovery. During the summer and fall of 1995, surveys showed that individuals from all four of the reintroduced species are surviving in Abrams Creek, and at least three of the four reintroduced species are reproducing!

The duskytail darter is part of the Abrams Creek ecosystem.
Dick Biggins/US FWS

Nearly 20 percent (168 species in 1996) of the species federally listed in the United States are found on the Service's National Wildlife Refuges. A total of 55 refuges have been established to support threatened and endangered species.

Cleaning vegetation from the sides of the creek allows the native aquatic vegetation to grow. This helps recover the listed species, because this vegetation is the food source for some of them.
D. Ledig/USFWS

Measuring stream flow at Ash Meadows National Wildlife Refuge helps to determine if there is enough water for the listed species.
Beth St. George/USFWS

Ash Meadows National Wildlife Refuge

One of the ways that the government assists with the recovery of listed species is to secure and protect habitat that is essential to a species' existence by establishing National Wildlife Refuges (NWR). Ash Meadows NWR is one of these protected areas. This specific refuge is a wetland ecosystem, which contains a system of natural seeps and springs in the Mohave Desert on the California/Nevada border. These seeps and springs enrich the desert environment and provide an excellent example of a desert oasis, which is extremely uncommon. The most significant benefit provided by Ash Meadows NWR is the protection of a truly unique environment that endangered and threatened species and a variety of other wildlife depend upon for habitat. This refuge provides habitat for at least 24 plants and animals found nowhere else in the world; 12 of these are listed species. The listed species include: four species of fish, seven plants, and one aquatic insect.

The Devil's Hole pupfish has been protected by establishing the Ash Meadows National Wildlife Refuge.
Photo: USFWS

The Ash Meadows ecosystem is home to 24 species found nowhere else, such as the Ash Meadows speckled dace and the Ash Meadows milk vetch.
USFWS

Since passage of the Act, 1,090 species have been listed in the United States as either endangered or threatened, and, for all but seven, extinction has been prevented.

Karner Blue Butterfly

The fate of this azure blue butterfly is tied to natural fires that, prior to European settlement, periodically swept through dry, sandy pine and oak-pine forests creating sunlit openings just right for an explosion of the butterfly's food plant, the equally blue, wild lupine. Recovery efforts for this butterfly are occurring in numerous States. The range of the Karner blue butterfly spans several States and the Canadian Province of Ontario, with the majority of the butterfly populations occurring in Wisconsin and Michigan. Other States with butterfly occurrences include Minnesota, Indiana, New York, and New Hampshire. Locations include private and public lands, forests, power lines corridors, and road rights-of-way. Historically, the butterfly also was found in Illinois, Massachusetts, Ohio, and Pennsylvania, although these populations are likely extirpated.

The Wisconsin Department of Natural Resources has taken the lead on developing a statewide Habitat Conservation Plan that will help conserve the Karner blue butterfly. It will allow for ecosystem planning to recover the species, while helping other species that depend on the same habitat. Forestry practices have had a great impact upon the butterfly. Harvesting of some diseased trees is being delayed because of the possible threat to the butterfly. The Wisconsin DNR, various county foresters, Georgia Pacific Corp., Consolidated Papers Inc., utilities, and private landowners currently are working on a plan to help recover the species and allow timber harvesting to occur.

The Service also is working with a number of partners on projects and activities to protect and manage habitat for the Karner blue butterfly in New York and New Hampshire. Partners in these efforts include the New York State Department of Environmental Conservation; the New Hampshire Fish and Game Department; The Nature Conservancy; the Albany Pine Bush Preserve Commission; other State, Federal, and local agencies and governments; private companies; and private landowners. Ongoing management activities include tree and brush removal, mowing, prescribed burning, planting wild lupine and other plant species that provide nectar sources for the adult butterflies, and collection and storage of lupine and nectar species seeds. A Karner blue butterfly captive rearing program also has been undertaken in New Hampshire to attempt to increase the size of its population.

Recovery efforts for the swamp pink include habitat protection and pollution control.
USFWS

Swamp Pink

Cleaning up polluted groundwater at a landfill site in New Jersey could have posed a threat to the swamp pink, because this could have dried up the wetlands upon which this threatened wildflower depends. But with help from the Service, the cleanup design was altered to protect habitat for 25,000 clumps of the swamp pink, while still allowing for capture of the contaminated water.

West Indian Manatee

Radio- and satellite-tracking of manatees continues to provide information on migration routes and essential manatee habitat. Researchers also are conducting studies related to the reproductive rates for manatees. In addition, the Manatee sanctuaries at the Crystal River and Merritt Island National Wildlife Refuges have been expanded as a sanctuary for these gentle sea-cows, and sick, injured, and orphaned manatees continue to be rescued.

Research on migration routes and reproduction rates of the West Indian manatee will help alleviate those problems that affect this species.
USFWS

Can Private Individuals Become Involved in Recovering Species?

Yes! Everyone can make a difference in the conservation and recovery of plants and animals. Many private landowners are helping to recover species through habitat improvement projects on their land. The Service helps in these efforts by providing technical assistance and through "safe harbor" agreements with landowners. A safe harbor agreement assures landowners that improving habitat for species will not restrict land-use options on their land in the future. Your State's natural resources or fish and wildlife agencies also should be able to help you determine if there are threatened or endangered species in your area and what you can do to help conserve or recover the species. Ordinary citizens, whether or not they own land, also may be able to become involved in the recovery of a listed species through activities sponsored by non-governmental groups in their area. There is usually a wide range of recovery activities, requiring diverse talents and interests, that need to be implemented, from field work (e.g., planting native plants) to office work (e.g., helping with public outreach) to assist in recovering listed species. Before beginning a new recovery project, individuals and groups should check with the appropriate State or Federal agency to ensure that their efforts are part of a coordinated strategy.

You can make a difference when it comes to recovering threatened and endangered species! To find out more about partnership opportunities for threatened and endangered species recovery, contact a Service office in your area.

Green Pitcher-plant

Because of recovery efforts, the numbers of endangered green pitcher-plants recently have increased at several locations. Several populations also now receive permanent protection, because the land has been set aside through a land acquisition program by The Nature Conservancy. Additionally, 13 other populations have short-term security through voluntary Conservation Agreements between private landowners and conservation groups, State natural resource agencies, and local land trust organizations.

Gray Wolf

Gray wolves in Minnesota, as well as in nearby Michigan and Wisconsin, are doing well under the protection of the Act. A program monitoring the numbers and range of these animals indicates that they are well on their way to recovery. Minnesota's wolf population is estimated to be around 2,000 animals. The population of wolves in Michigan and Wisconsin has been increasing in recent years. In late winter 1995-1996, state wolf biologists estimated a population of 102 to 110 wolves in Michigan's Upper Peninsula. This number does not include another 22 wolves found within Isle Royale National Park in Lake Superior.

The California condor was reintroduced into the wild, thanks to recovery efforts from many partners. [photo]/USFWS

California Condor

As late as the mid-1980's, the California condor teetered on the brink of extinction. By 1987, the Service had collected the few remaining wild condors as an emergency measure to save the species from extinction through captive propagation. Through the recovery program, 26 captive-bred condors are now flying freely in the skies of southern California, Utah, and Arizona.

Tagging bald eagle chicks are part of ongoing recovery monitoring efforts that are conducted to check the status of the populations.

How Can I Get More Information About Endangered Species?

The Service's Division of Endangered Species maintains a Home Page on the Internet's World Wide Web, designed to offer exciting graphics, comprehensive information on threatened and endangered species, and specific geographic information from the Service's Regional and Field Offices. The Endangered Species's Home Page can be found at http://www.fws.gov. Once there, within the list of contents, click on "Nationwide Activities," then "Endangered Species Home Page." This Internet address provides some of the most current information available on threatened and endangered species and related programs.

You also can find additional information in the publication, *The 1994 Report to Congress: Endangered and Threatened Species Recovery Program*, which can be purchased from the U.S. Government Printing Office, Superintendent of Documents, Mail Stop: SSOP, Washington, D.C. 20402-9328. The cost of the report is $4.50 and the order number is S/N02401000712-5. Additionally, *The 1996 Report to Congress* should be out in the Fall of 1997.

Also, the University of Michigan publishes the *Endangered Species Update*, a newsletter that includes reprints of the Service's *Endangered Species Bulletin*. For more information write the Endangered Species *Update*, School of Natural Resources, University of Michigan, Ann Arbor, Michigan 48109-1115, or call (313) 763-3243.

Right: The golden-cheeked warbler is one of seven species protected by planning efforts in Travis County, Texas.
Steve Maslowski/USFWS

Golden-Cheeked Warbler

Through habitat conservation planning activities for the golden-cheeked warbler in Texas, 4,600 acres of habitat are being protected. Travis County, the City of Austin, the Nature Conservancy of Texas, Texas Parks and Wildlife Department, Audubon Society, the Service, and others worked together on a comprehensive habitat conservation plan for a total of seven endangered species in the Austin, Texas, area.

Myrtle's Silverspot Butterfly

One population of Myrtle's silverspot butterfly is protected on Point Reyes National Seashore. Management at the seashore includes control of introduced plants that crowd out native plant species needed by the butterfly.

Summary

Habitat degradation and destruction over three centuries have brought many plants and animals to the brink of extinction, but successful recovery efforts can reverse these declines when everyone works together. One of the key ingredients to recovery is the cooperation of many partners working together to develop innovative conservation and management actions that benefit the species, while accommodating socioeconomic goals. For species after species, this collaborative approach to the recovery process has brought together partners as diverse as State and foreign governments, major corporations, grassroots conservation organizations, and private landowners to improve the habitat for imperiled plants and animals and for ourselves. We have been largely successful in meeting these challenges. Both the species and the people involved in recovery benefit from conserving and restoring habitat.

Thanks to cooperative recovery programs, the bald eagle once can again be seen soaring over much of our country, and gray wolves again can be heard howling in the Northern Rockies. With persistence and time, it is possible to reverse the decline of many more species and to support them along the road to recovery. When we all participate in conservation, our precious natural environment can be protected in ways that benefit everyone.

U.S. Fish & Wildlife Service

WASHINGTON D.C. OFFICE *Washington, D.C. 20240*

Jamie Rappaport Clark, *Director*
Sam Hamilton,
   Acting Assistant Director for Ecological Services

E. LaVerne Smith, *Chief, Division of Endangered Species*	(703)358-2171
Ren Lohoefener, *Deputy Chief, Division of Endangered Species*	(703)358-2171
Lesli Gray, *Acting Chief, Branch of Information Management*	(703)358-2390
Jay Slack, *Chief, Branch of Conservation and Classification*	(703)358-2105
Richard Hannan, *Chief, Branch of Recovery & Consultation*	(703)358-2106
	http://www.fws.gov

REGION ONE *Eastside Federal Complex, 911 N.E.11th Ave, Portland OR 97232*

California, Hawaii, Idaho, Nevada, Oregon, Washington, American Samoa, Commonwealth of the Northern Mariana Islands, Guam and the Pacific Trust Territories

Michael J. Spear, *Regional Director*

(503)231-6118
http://www.r1.fws.gov

REGION TWO *P.O. Box 1306, Albuquerque, NM 87103*

Arizona, New Mexico, Oklahoma, and Texas

Nancy Kaufman, *Regional Director*

(505)248-6282
http://sturgeon.irm1.r2.fws.gov

REGION THREE *Federal Bldg., Ft. Snelling, Twin Cities MN 55111*

Illinois, Indiana, Iowa, Michigan, Minnesota, Missouri, Ohio, and Wisconsin

William Hartwig, *Regional Director*

(612)725-3500
http://www.fws.gov/~r3pao/r3home.html

REGION FOUR *1875 Century Blvd., Suite 200, Atlanta, GA 30345*

Alabama, Arkansas, Louisiana, Georgia, Kentucky, Mississippi, North Carolina, South Carolina, Florida, Tennessee, Puerto Rico, and the U.S. Virgin Islands

Dale Hall, *Acting Regional Director*

(404)679-4000
http://www.fws.gov/~r4eao

REGION FIVE *300 Westgate Center Drive, Hadley, MA 01035*

Connecticut, Delaware, District of Columbia, Maine, Maryland, Massachusetts, New Hampshire, New Jersey, New York, Pennsylvania, Rhode Island, Vermont, Virginia, and West Virginia

Ronald E. Lambertson, *Regional Director*

(413)253-8659
http://www.fws.gov/~r5fws

REGION SIX *P.O. Box 25486, Denver Federal Center, Denver CO 80225*

Colorado, Kansas, Montana, Nebraska, North Dakota, South Dakota, Utah, and Wyoming

Ralph O. Morgenweck, *Regional Director*

(303)236-7920
http://www.r6.fws.gov/www/fws

REGION SEVEN *1011 E. Tudor Rd., Anchorage, AK 99503*

Alaska

Dave Allen, *Regional Director*

(907)786-3542
http://www.fws.gov/~r7hpirm

"This is the *legacy I would like to leave behind:* I would like to stop the ridicule about the conservation of snails, lichens, and fungi, and instead, move the debate to which ecosystems are the most recoverable, and how we can save them, making room for them and ourselves."

Mollie H. Beattie

Director, U.S. Fish and

Wildlife Service

1993-1996

Below:
Wood Stork chicks
USFWS

Back Cover:
Sunset on Pacific
Paul Benvenuti/USFWS

U.S. Department of the Interior

Fish and Wildlife Service